2022

RUNNING PLANNER

THIS BELONGS TO

PHONE NUMBER

ABOUT THIS BOOK

Whether you run for fun, fitness, or competition, keeping track of your runs is a great way to measure improvement and continually motivate yourself.

This running planner contains everything needed for a runner, from beginner to professional and for everyone in between. We understand that each individual will have different needs, so feel free to use this book how best suits you. You may decide to leave some section blank (E.g. heart rate and calories if fitness is not your goal), and there are plenty of lined notes pages at the back of the book should you require space for something not tracked in this book.

A list of items included of this book includes:

- **2022 Year at a glance calendar** with space for noting down important dates for the year
- **2022 Monthly calendar** (2 Page spread)
- **Weekly / daily calendar** with space each day for notes about your run, as well inputs for Distance, Time, Pace, Heart rate and Calories burned.
- **Total distance tracker** to add up distance run over the year
- **Goals checklist** - What are your personal goals for the year?
- **Goal race list** - Which races would you like to attend this year? Includes location and date
- **Race results** - Track your pace, distance, time and placement for each race you compete in
- **Yearly reflection** - Space for you to reflect on the year with suggestions on topics to write about.
- **Lined notes pages** with date, for you to use how best fits your needs.

We suggest having a good look through the book before using it, to ensure you know which elements of your running journey to keep note of! On the next page is a sample of **some** of the pages contained in this book.

2022 CALENDAR

January
February
March
April
May
June

IMPORTANT DATES

DATE	DESCRIPTION

YEARLY RECAP

Total Distance Run	
Longest Run	
Number of Runs	
Number of Races Run	
Total Distance (Race)	
Quickest Pace (Race)	
Best Placement in a Race	
Average Race Placement	
Longest Weekly Distance	
Longest Monthly Distance	

JANUARY

MONDAY	TUESDAY	WEDNESDAY	THURSDAY
27	28	29	30
3	4	5	6
10	11	12	13
17	18	19	20
24	25	26	27
31	1	2	3

FRIDAY	SATURDAY	SUNDAY	NOTES
31	1	2	
7	8	9	
14	15	16	
21	22	23	
28	29	30	
4	5	6	

MY RACE RESULTS

DATE	DISTANCE	TIME	PACE	PLACE

December 27, 2022 >> January 2, 2022 — Week 1

Monday 27 December	
Tuesday 28 December	
Wednesday 29 December	
Thursday 30 December	
Friday 31 December	
Saturday 1 January	
Sunday 2 January	

NOTES:

January 3, 2022 >> January 9, 2022 — Week 2

Monday 3 January	
Tuesday 4 January	
Wednesday 5 January	
Thursday 6 January	
Friday 7 January	
Saturday 8 January	
Sunday 9 January	

NOTES:

NOTES

DATE	NOTE

January

M	T	W	T	F	S	S
					1	2
3	4	5	6	7	8	9
10	11	12	13	14	15	16
17	18	19	20	21	22	23
24	25	26	27	28	29	30
31						

February

M	T	W	T	F	S	S
	1	2	3	4	5	6
7	8	9	10	11	12	13
14	15	16	17	18	19	20
21	22	23	24	25	26	27
28						

March

M	T	W	T	F	S	S
	1	2	3	4	5	6
7	8	9	10	11	12	13
14	15	16	17	18	19	20
21	22	23	24	25	26	27
28	29	30	31			

April

M	T	W	T	F	S	S
				1	2	3
4	5	6	7	8	9	10
11	12	13	14	15	16	17
18	19	20	21	22	23	24
25	26	27	28	29	30	

May

M	T	W	T	F	S	S
						1
2	3	4	5	6	7	8
9	10	11	12	13	14	15
16	17	18	19	20	21	22
23	24	25	26	27	28	29
30	31					

June

M	T	W	T	F	S	S
		1	2	3	4	5
6	7	8	9	10	11	12
13	14	15	16	17	18	19
20	21	22	23	24	25	26
27	28	29	30			

DATE	DESCRIPTION

July

M	T	W	T	F	S	S
				1	2	3
4	5	6	7	8	9	10
11	12	13	14	15	16	17
18	19	20	21	22	23	24
25	26	27	28	29	30	31

August

M	T	W	T	F	S	S
1	2	3	4	5	6	7
8	9	10	11	12	13	14
15	16	17	18	19	20	21
22	23	24	25	26	27	28
29	30	31				

September

M	T	W	T	F	S	S
			1	2	3	4
5	6	7	8	9	10	11
12	13	14	15	16	17	18
19	20	21	22	23	24	25
26	27	28	29	30		

October

M	T	W	T	F	S	S
					1	2
3	4	5	6	7	8	9
10	11	12	13	14	15	16
17	18	19	20	21	22	23
24	25	26	27	28	29	30
31						

November

M	T	W	T	F	S	S
	1	2	3	4	5	6
7	8	9	10	11	12	13
14	15	16	17	18	19	20
21	22	23	24	25	26	27
28	29	30	1	2	3	4

December

M	T	W	T	F	S	S
28	29	30	1	2	3	4
5	6	7	8	9	10	11
12	13	14	15	16	17	18
19	20	21	22	23	24	25
26	27	28	29	30	31	

DATE	DESCRIPTION

GOALS

GOAL	X	DATE ACHIEVED
Keep good pace		

GOAL	X	DATE ACHIEVED

DATE	RACE	RACE LOCATION	X
5-8-22	Mother's Day	Dryden Lake Park	
5-21-22	Steph's Run	Borg Warner	
6-19-22	Dermott Race	Ithaca Cass Park	
10-15-22	YMCA 5K series	Yaman Park, Courtland	
11-27-22	Ugly Sweater 5K	Dryden Nature Trail	
3-11-23	St. Patrick's 4 Miler	Binghamton	
5-7-23	Mountain Goat 10 Miler	Syracuse	

DATE	RACE	RACE LOCATION	X

MY RACE RESULTS

DATE	DISTANCE	TIME	PACE	PLACE

MY RACE RESULTS

DATE	DISTANCE	TIME	PACE	PLACE

MONDAY	TUESDAY	WEDNESDAY	THURSDAY
27	28	29	30
3	4	5	6
10	11	12	13
17	18	19	20
24	25	26	27
31	1	2	3

FRIDAY	SATURDAY	SUNDAY	NOTES
31	1	2	
7	8	9	
14	15	16	
21	22	23	
28	29	30	
4	5	6	

FEBRUARY

MONDAY	TUESDAY	WEDNESDAY	THURSDAY
31	1	2	3
7	8	9	10
14	15	16	17
21	22	23	24
28	1	2	3

FRIDAY	SATURDAY	SUNDAY	NOTES
4	5	6	
11	12	13	
18	19	20	
25	26	27	
4	5	6	

MONDAY	TUESDAY	WEDNESDAY	THURSDAY
28	1	2	3
7	8	9	10
14	15	16	17
21	22	23	24
28	29	30	31

FRIDAY	SATURDAY	SUNDAY	NOTES
4	5	6	
11	12	13	
18	19	20	
25	26	27	
1	2	3	

MONDAY	TUESDAY	WEDNESDAY	THURSDAY
28	29	30	31
4	5	6	7
11	12	13	14
18	19	20	21
25	26	27	28

FRIDAY	SATURDAY	SUNDAY	NOTES
1	2	3	
8	9	10	
15	16	17	
22	23	24	
29	30	1	

MONDAY	TUESDAY	WEDNESDAY	THURSDAY
25	26	27	28
2	3	4	5
9	10	11	12
16	17	18	19
23	24	25	26
30	31	1	2

FRIDAY	SATURDAY	SUNDAY	NOTES
29	30	1	
6	7	8	
13	14	15	
20	21	22	
27	28	29	
3	4	5	

MONDAY	TUESDAY	WEDNESDAY	THURSDAY
30	31	1	2
6	7	8	9
13	14	15	16
20	21	22	23
27	28	29	30

FRIDAY	SATURDAY	SUNDAY	NOTES
3	4	5	
10	11	12	
17	18	19	
24	25	26	
1	2	3	

MONDAY	TUESDAY	WEDNESDAY	THURSDAY
27	28	29	30
4	5	6	7
11	12	13	14
18	19	20	21
25	26	27	28

FRIDAY	SATURDAY	SUNDAY	NOTES
1	2	3	
8	9	10	
15	16	17	
22	23	24	
29	30	31	

MONDAY	TUESDAY	WEDNESDAY	THURSDAY
1	2	3	4
8	9	10	11
15	16	17	18
22	23	24	25
29	30	31	1

FRIDAY	SATURDAY	SUNDAY	NOTES
5	6	7	
12	13	14	
19	20	21	
26	27	28	
2	3	4	

MONDAY	TUESDAY	WEDNESDAY	THURSDAY
29	30	31	1
5	6	7	8
12	13	14	15
19	20	21	22
26	27	28	29

FRIDAY	SATURDAY	SUNDAY	NOTES
2	3	4	
9	10	11	
16	17	18	
23	24	25	
30	1	2	

MONDAY	TUESDAY	WEDNESDAY	THURSDAY
26	27	28	29
3	4	5	6
10	11	12	13
17	18	19	20
24	25	26	27
31	1	2	3

FRIDAY	SATURDAY	SUNDAY	NOTES
30	1	2	
7	8	9	
14	15	16	
21	22	23	
28	29	30	
4	5	6	

MONDAY	TUESDAY	WEDNESDAY	THURSDAY
31	1	2	3
7	8	9	10
14	15	16	17
21	22	23	24
28	29	30	1

FRIDAY	SATURDAY	SUNDAY	NOTES
4	5	6	
11	12	13	
18	19	20	
25	26	27	
2	3	4	

DECEMBER

MONDAY	TUESDAY	WEDNESDAY	THURSDAY
28	29	30	1
5	6	7	8
12	13	14	15
19	20	21	22
26	27	28	29

FRIDAY	SATURDAY	SUNDAY	NOTES
2	3	4	
9	10	11	
16	17	18	
23	24	25	
30	31	1	

Monday **27** December		DISTANCE	
		TIME	
		PACE	
		HEART RATE	
		CALORIES	
Tuesday **28** December		DISTANCE	
		TIME	
		PACE	
		HEART RATE	
		CALORIES	
Wednesday **29** December		DISTANCE	
		TIME	
		PACE	
		HEART RATE	
		CALORIES	
Thursday **30** December		DISTANCE	
		TIME	
		PACE	
		HEART RATE	
		CALORIES	
Friday **31** December		DISTANCE	
		TIME	
		PACE	
		HEART RATE	
		CALORIES	
Saturday **1** January		DISTANCE	
		TIME	
		PACE	
		HEART RATE	
		CALORIES	
Sunday **2** January		DISTANCE	
		TIME	
		PACE	
		HEART RATE	
		CALORIES	

NOTES, ACHIEVEMENTS, EXTRA TRAINING

THIS WEEKS DISTANCE	
TOTAL YEARLY DISTANCE	

Monday **3** January		DISTANCE	
		TIME	
		PACE	
		HEART RATE	
		CALORIES	
Tuesday **4** January		DISTANCE	
		TIME	
		PACE	
		HEART RATE	
		CALORIES	
Wednesday **5** January		DISTANCE	
		TIME	
		PACE	
		HEART RATE	
		CALORIES	
Thursday **6** January		DISTANCE	
		TIME	
		PACE	
		HEART RATE	
		CALORIES	
Friday **7** January		DISTANCE	
		TIME	
		PACE	
		HEART RATE	
		CALORIES	
Saturday **8** January		DISTANCE	
		TIME	
		PACE	
		HEART RATE	
		CALORIES	
Sunday **9** January		DISTANCE	
		TIME	
		PACE	
		HEART RATE	
		CALORIES	

NOTES, ACHIEVEMENTS, EXTRA TRAINING

| THIS WEEKS DISTANCE | |
| TOTAL YEARLY DISTANCE | |

Monday 10 January		DISTANCE	
		TIME	
		PACE	
		HEART RATE	
		CALORIES	
Tuesday 11 January		DISTANCE	
		TIME	
		PACE	
		HEART RATE	
		CALORIES	
Wednesday 12 January		DISTANCE	
		TIME	
		PACE	
		HEART RATE	
		CALORIES	
Thursday 13 January		DISTANCE	
		TIME	
		PACE	
		HEART RATE	
		CALORIES	
Friday 14 January		DISTANCE	
		TIME	
		PACE	
		HEART RATE	
		CALORIES	
Saturday 15 January		DISTANCE	
		TIME	
		PACE	
		HEART RATE	
		CALORIES	
Sunday 16 January		DISTANCE	
		TIME	
		PACE	
		HEART RATE	
		CALORIES	

NOTES, ACHIEVEMENTS, EXTRA TRAINING

| THIS WEEKS DISTANCE | |
| TOTAL YEARLY DISTANCE | |

Monday **17** January		DISTANCE	
		TIME	
		PACE	
		HEART RATE	
		CALORIES	
Tuesday **18** January		DISTANCE	
		TIME	
		PACE	
		HEART RATE	
		CALORIES	
Wednesday **19** January		DISTANCE	
		TIME	
		PACE	
		HEART RATE	
		CALORIES	
Thursday **20** January		DISTANCE	
		TIME	
		PACE	
		HEART RATE	
		CALORIES	
Friday **21** January		DISTANCE	
		TIME	
		PACE	
		HEART RATE	
		CALORIES	
Saturday **22** January		DISTANCE	
		TIME	
		PACE	
		HEART RATE	
		CALORIES	
Sunday **23** January		DISTANCE	
		TIME	
		PACE	
		HEART RATE	
		CALORIES	

NOTES, ACHIEVEMENTS, EXTRA TRAINING

THIS WEEKS DISTANCE	
TOTAL YEARLY DISTANCE	

Monday **24** January		DISTANCE	
		TIME	
		PACE	
		HEART RATE	
		CALORIES	

Tuesday **25** January		DISTANCE	
		TIME	
		PACE	
		HEART RATE	
		CALORIES	

Wednesday **26** January		DISTANCE	
		TIME	
		PACE	
		HEART RATE	
		CALORIES	

Thursday **27** January		DISTANCE	
		TIME	
		PACE	
		HEART RATE	
		CALORIES	

Friday **28** January		DISTANCE	
		TIME	
		PACE	
		HEART RATE	
		CALORIES	

Saturday **29** January		DISTANCE	
		TIME	
		PACE	
		HEART RATE	
		CALORIES	

Sunday **30** January		DISTANCE	
		TIME	
		PACE	
		HEART RATE	
		CALORIES	

NOTES, ACHIEVEMENTS, EXTRA TRAINING

| THIS WEEKS DISTANCE | |
| TOTAL YEARLY DISTANCE | |

Monday **31** January		DISTANCE	
		TIME	
		PACE	
		HEART RATE	
		CALORIES	
Tuesday **1** February		DISTANCE	
		TIME	
		PACE	
		HEART RATE	
		CALORIES	
Wednesday **2** February		DISTANCE	
		TIME	
		PACE	
		HEART RATE	
		CALORIES	
Thursday **3** February		DISTANCE	
		TIME	
		PACE	
		HEART RATE	
		CALORIES	
Friday **4** February		DISTANCE	
		TIME	
		PACE	
		HEART RATE	
		CALORIES	
Saturday **5** February		DISTANCE	
		TIME	
		PACE	
		HEART RATE	
		CALORIES	
Sunday **6** February		DISTANCE	
		TIME	
		PACE	
		HEART RATE	
		CALORIES	

NOTES, ACHIEVEMENTS, EXTRA TRAINING

| THIS WEEKS DISTANCE | |
| TOTAL YEARLY DISTANCE | |

Monday **7** February		DISTANCE	
		TIME	
		PACE	
		HEART RATE	
		CALORIES	
Tuesday **8** February		DISTANCE	
		TIME	
		PACE	
		HEART RATE	
		CALORIES	
Wednesday **9** February		DISTANCE	
		TIME	
		PACE	
		HEART RATE	
		CALORIES	
Thursday **10** February		DISTANCE	
		TIME	
		PACE	
		HEART RATE	
		CALORIES	
Friday **11** February		DISTANCE	
		TIME	
		PACE	
		HEART RATE	
		CALORIES	
Saturday **12** February		DISTANCE	
		TIME	
		PACE	
		HEART RATE	
		CALORIES	
Sunday **13** February		DISTANCE	
		TIME	
		PACE	
		HEART RATE	
		CALORIES	

NOTES, ACHIEVEMENTS, EXTRA TRAINING

THIS WEEKS DISTANCE	
TOTAL YEARLY DISTANCE	

Monday **14** February		DISTANCE	
		TIME	
		PACE	
		HEART RATE	
		CALORIES	
Tuesday **15** February		DISTANCE	
		TIME	
		PACE	
		HEART RATE	
		CALORIES	
Wednesday **16** February		DISTANCE	
		TIME	
		PACE	
		HEART RATE	
		CALORIES	
Thursday **17** February		DISTANCE	
		TIME	
		PACE	
		HEART RATE	
		CALORIES	
Friday **18** February		DISTANCE	
		TIME	
		PACE	
		HEART RATE	
		CALORIES	
Saturday **19** February		DISTANCE	
		TIME	
		PACE	
		HEART RATE	
		CALORIES	
Sunday **20** February		DISTANCE	
		TIME	
		PACE	
		HEART RATE	
		CALORIES	

NOTES, ACHIEVEMENTS, EXTRA TRAINING

| THIS WEEKS DISTANCE | |
| TOTAL YEARLY DISTANCE | |

Monday **21** February		DISTANCE	
		TIME	
		PACE	
		HEART RATE	
		CALORIES	
Tuesday **22** February		DISTANCE	
		TIME	
		PACE	
		HEART RATE	
		CALORIES	
Wednesday **23** February		DISTANCE	
		TIME	
		PACE	
		HEART RATE	
		CALORIES	
Thursday **24** February		DISTANCE	
		TIME	
		PACE	
		HEART RATE	
		CALORIES	
Friday **25** February		DISTANCE	
		TIME	
		PACE	
		HEART RATE	
		CALORIES	
Saturday **26** February		DISTANCE	
		TIME	
		PACE	
		HEART RATE	
		CALORIES	
Sunday **27** February		DISTANCE	
		TIME	
		PACE	
		HEART RATE	
		CALORIES	

NOTES, ACHIEVEMENTS, EXTRA TRAINING

| THIS WEEKS DISTANCE | |
| TOTAL YEARLY DISTANCE | |

Monday **28** February		DISTANCE	
		TIME	
		PACE	
		HEART RATE	
		CALORIES	
Tuesday **1** March		DISTANCE	
		TIME	
		PACE	
		HEART RATE	
		CALORIES	
Wednesday **2** March		DISTANCE	
		TIME	
		PACE	
		HEART RATE	
		CALORIFS	
Thursday **3** March		DISTANCE	
		TIME	
		PACE	
		HEART RATE	
		CALORIES	
Friday **4** March		DISTANCE	
		TIME	
		PACE	
		HEART RATE	
		CALORIES	
Saturday **5** March		DISTANCE	
		TIME	
		PACE	
		HEART RATE	
		CALORIES	
Sunday **6** March		DISTANCE	
		TIME	
		PACE	
		HEART RATE	
		CALORIES	

NOTES, ACHIEVEMENTS, EXTRA TRAINING

| THIS WEEKS DISTANCE | |
| TOTAL YEARLY DISTANCE | |

Monday **7** March		DISTANCE	
		TIME	
		PACE	
		HEART RATE	
		CALORIES	
Tuesday **8** March		DISTANCE	
		TIME	
		PACE	
		HEART RATE	
		CALORIES	
Wednesday **9** March		DISTANCE	
		TIME	
		PACE	
		HEART RATE	
		CALORIES	
Thursday **10** March		DISTANCE	
		TIME	
		PACE	
		HEART RATE	
		CALORIES	
Friday **11** March		DISTANCE	
		TIME	
		PACE	
		HEART RATE	
		CALORIES	
Saturday **12** March		DISTANCE	
		TIME	
		PACE	
		HEART RATE	
		CALORIES	
Sunday **13** March		DISTANCE	
		TIME	
		PACE	
		HEART RATE	
		CALORIES	

NOTES, ACHIEVEMENTS, EXTRA TRAINING

| THIS WEEKS DISTANCE | |
| TOTAL YEARLY DISTANCE | |

Monday **14** March		DISTANCE	
		TIME	
		PACE	
		HEART RATE	
		CALORIES	
Tuesday **15** March		DISTANCE	
		TIME	
		PACE	
		HEART RATE	
		CALORIES	
Wednesday **16** March		DISTANCE	
		TIME	
		PACE	
		HEART RATE	
		CALORIES	
Thursday **17** March		DISTANCE	
		TIME	
		PACE	
		HEART RATE	
		CALORIES	
Friday **18** March		DISTANCE	
		TIME	
		PACE	
		HEART RATE	
		CALORIES	
Saturday **19** March		DISTANCE	
		TIME	
		PACE	
		HEART RATE	
		CALORIES	
Sunday **20** March		DISTANCE	
		TIME	
		PACE	
		HEART RATE	
		CALORIES	

NOTES, ACHIEVEMENTS, EXTRA TRAINING

| THIS WEEKS DISTANCE | |
| TOTAL YEARLY DISTANCE | |

Monday **21** March		DISTANCE	
		TIME	
		PACE	
		HEART RATE	
		CALORIES	
Tuesday **22** March		DISTANCE	
		TIME	
		PACE	
		HEART RATE	
		CALORIES	
Wednesday **23** March		DISTANCE	
		TIME	
		PACE	
		HEART RATE	
		CALORIES	
Thursday **24** March		DISTANCE	
		TIME	
		PACE	
		HEART RATE	
		CALORIES	
Friday **25** March		DISTANCE	
		TIME	
		PACE	
		HEART RATE	
		CALORIES	
Saturday **26** March		DISTANCE	
		TIME	
		PACE	
		HEART RATE	
		CALORIES	
Sunday **27** March		DISTANCE	
		TIME	
		PACE	
		HEART RATE	
		CALORIES	

NOTES, ACHIEVEMENTS, EXTRA TRAINING

| THIS WEEKS DISTANCE | |
| TOTAL YEARLY DISTANCE | |

Monday **28** March		DISTANCE	
		TIME	
		PACE	
		HEART RATE	
		CALORIES	
Tuesday **29** March		DISTANCE	
		TIME	
		PACE	
		HEART RATE	
		CALORIES	
Wednesday **30** March		DISTANCE	
		TIME	
		PACE	
		HEART RATE	
		CALORIES	
Thursday **31** March		DISTANCE	
		TIME	
		PACE	
		HEART RATE	
		CALORIES	
Friday **1** April		DISTANCE	
		TIME	
		PACE	
		HEART RATE	
		CALORIES	
Saturday **2** April		DISTANCE	
		TIME	
		PACE	
		HEART RATE	
		CALORIES	
Sunday **3** April		DISTANCE	
		TIME	
		PACE	
		HEART RATE	
		CALORIES	

NOTES, ACHIEVEMENTS, EXTRA TRAINING

THIS WEEKS DISTANCE	
TOTAL YEARLY DISTANCE	

Monday **4** April		DISTANCE	
		TIME	
		PACE	
		HEART RATE	
		CALORIES	
Tuesday **5** April		DISTANCE	
		TIME	
		PACE	
		HEART RATE	
		CALORIES	
Wednesday **6** April		DISTANCE	
		TIME	
		PACE	
		HEART RATE	
		CALORIES	
Thursday **7** April		DISTANCE	
		TIME	
		PACE	
		HEART RATE	
		CALORIES	
Friday **8** April		DISTANCE	
		TIME	
		PACE	
		HEART RATE	
		CALORIES	
Saturday **9** April		DISTANCE	
		TIME	
		PACE	
		HEART RATE	
		CALORIES	
Sunday **10** April		DISTANCE	
		TIME	
		PACE	
		HEART RATE	
		CALORIES	

NOTES, ACHIEVEMENTS, EXTRA TRAINING

| THIS WEEKS DISTANCE | |
| TOTAL YEARLY DISTANCE | |

Monday **11** April		DISTANCE	
		TIME	
		PACE	
		HEART RATE	
		CALORIES	
Tuesday **12** April		DISTANCE	
		TIME	
		PACE	
		HEART RATE	
		CALORIES	
Wednesday **13** April		DISTANCE	
		TIME	
		PACE	
		HEART RATE	
		CALORIES	
Thursday **14** April		DISTANCE	
		TIME	
		PACE	
		HEART RATE	
		CALORIES	
Friday **15** April		DISTANCE	
		TIME	
		PACE	
		HEART RATE	
		CALORIES	
Saturday **16** April		DISTANCE	
		TIME	
		PACE	
		HEART RATE	
		CALORIES	
Sunday **17** April		DISTANCE	
		TIME	
		PACE	
		HEART RATE	
		CALORIES	

NOTES, ACHIEVEMENTS, EXTRA TRAINING

| THIS WEEKS DISTANCE | |
| TOTAL YEARLY DISTANCE | |

Monday **18** April		DISTANCE	
		TIME	
		PACE	
		HEART RATE	
		CALORIES	
Tuesday **19** April		DISTANCE	
		TIME	
		PACE	
		HEART RATE	
		CALORIES	
Wednesday **20** April		DISTANCE	
		TIME	
		PACE	
		HEART RATE	
		CALORIES	
Thursday **21** April		DISTANCE	
		TIME	
		PACE	
		HEART RATE	
		CALORIES	
Friday **22** April		DISTANCE	
		TIME	
		PACE	
		HEART RATE	
		CALORIES	
Saturday **23** April		DISTANCE	
		TIME	
		PACE	
		HEART RATE	
		CALORIES	
Sunday **24** April		DISTANCE	
		TIME	
		PACE	
		HEART RATE	
		CALORIES	

NOTES, ACHIEVEMENTS, EXTRA TRAINING

| THIS WEEKS DISTANCE | |
| TOTAL YEARLY DISTANCE | |

Monday **25** April		DISTANCE	
		TIME	
		PACE	
		HEART RATE	
		CALORIES	

Tuesday **26** April		DISTANCE	
		TIME	
		PACE	
		HEART RATE	
		CALORIES	

Wednesday **27** April		DISTANCE	
		TIME	
		PACE	
		HEART RATE	
		CALORIES	

Thursday **28** April		DISTANCE	
		TIME	
		PACE	
		HEART RATE	
		CALORIES	

Friday **29** April		DISTANCE	
		TIME	
		PACE	
		HEART RATE	
		CALORIES	

Saturday **30** April		DISTANCE	
		TIME	
		PACE	
		HEART RATE	
		CALORIES	

Sunday **1** May		DISTANCE	
		TIME	
		PACE	
		HEART RATE	
		CALORIES	

NOTES, ACHIEVEMENTS, EXTRA TRAINING

THIS WEEKS DISTANCE	
TOTAL YEARLY DISTANCE	

Monday 2 May		DISTANCE	
		TIME	
		PACE	
		HEART RATE	
		CALORIES	

Tuesday 3 May		DISTANCE	
		TIME	
		PACE	
		HEART RATE	
		CALORIES	

Wednesday 4 May		DISTANCE	
		TIME	
		PACE	
		HEART RATE	
		CALORIES	

Thursday 5 May		DISTANCE	
		TIME	
		PACE	
		HEART RATE	
		CALORIES	

Friday 6 May		DISTANCE	
		TIME	
		PACE	
		HEART RATE	
		CALORIES	

Saturday 7 May		DISTANCE	
		TIME	
		PACE	
		HEART RATE	
		CALORIES	

Sunday 8 May		DISTANCE	
		TIME	
		PACE	
		HEART RATE	
		CALORIES	

NOTES, ACHIEVEMENTS, EXTRA TRAINING

THIS WEEKS DISTANCE	
TOTAL YEARLY DISTANCE	

Monday **9** May		DISTANCE	
		TIME	
		PACE	
		HEART RATE	
		CALORIES	

Tuesday **10** May		DISTANCE	
		TIME	
		PACE	
		HEART RATE	
		CALORIES	

Wednesday **11** May		DISTANCE	
		TIME	
		PACE	
		HEART RATE	
		CALORIES	

Thursday **12** May		DISTANCE	
		TIME	
		PACE	
		HEART RATE	
		CALORIES	

Friday **13** May		DISTANCE	
		TIME	
		PACE	
		HEART RATE	
		CALORIES	

Saturday **14** May		DISTANCE	
		TIME	
		PACE	
		HEART RATE	
		CALORIES	

Sunday **15** May		DISTANCE	
		TIME	
		PACE	
		HEART RATE	
		CALORIES	

NOTES, ACHIEVEMENTS, EXTRA TRAINING

THIS WEEKS DISTANCE	
TOTAL YEARLY DISTANCE	

Monday **16** May		DISTANCE	
		TIME	
		PACE	
		HEART RATE	
		CALORIES	
Tuesday **17** May		DISTANCE	
		TIME	
		PACE	
		HEART RATE	
		CALORIES	
Wednesday **18** May		DISTANCE	
		TIME	
		PACE	
		HEART RATE	
		CALORIES	
Thursday **19** May		DISTANCE	
		TIME	
		PACE	
		HEART RATE	
		CALORIES	
Friday **20** May		DISTANCE	
		TIME	
		PACE	
		HEART RATE	
		CALORIES	
Saturday **21** May		DISTANCE	
		TIME	
		PACE	
		HEART RATE	
		CALORIES	
Sunday **22** May		DISTANCE	
		TIME	
		PACE	
		HEART RATE	
		CALORIES	

NOTES, ACHIEVEMENTS, EXTRA TRAINING

THIS WEEKS DISTANCE	
TOTAL YEARLY DISTANCE	

Monday **23** May		DISTANCE	
		TIME	
		PACE	
		HEART RATE	
		CALORIES	
Tuesday **24** May		DISTANCE	
		TIME	
		PACE	
		HEART RATE	
		CALORIES	
Wednesday **25** May		DISTANCE	
		TIME	
		PACE	
		HEART RATE	
		CALORIES	
Thursday **26** May		DISTANCE	
		TIME	
		PACE	
		HEART RATE	
		CALORIES	
Friday **27** May		DISTANCE	
		TIME	
		PACE	
		HEART RATE	
		CALORIES	
Saturday **28** May		DISTANCE	
		TIME	
		PACE	
		HEART RATE	
		CALORIES	
Sunday **29** May		DISTANCE	
		TIME	
		PACE	
		HEART RATE	
		CALORIES	

NOTES, ACHIEVEMENTS, EXTRA TRAINING

| THIS WEEKS DISTANCE | |
| TOTAL YEARLY DISTANCE | |

Monday **30** May		DISTANCE	
		TIME	
		PACE	
		HEART RATE	
		CALORIES	

Tuesday **31** May		DISTANCE	
		TIME	
		PACE	
		HEART RATE	
		CALORIES	

Wednesday **1** June		DISTANCE	
		TIME	
		PACE	
		HEART RATE	
		CALORIES	

Thursday **2** June		DISTANCE	
		TIME	
		PACE	
		HEART RATE	
		CALORIES	

Friday **3** June		DISTANCE	
		TIME	
		PACE	
		HEART RATE	
		CALORIES	

Saturday **4** June		DISTANCE	
		TIME	
		PACE	
		HEART RATE	
		CALORIES	

Sunday **5** June		DISTANCE	
		TIME	
		PACE	
		HEART RATE	
		CALORIES	

NOTES, ACHIEVEMENTS, EXTRA TRAINING

| THIS WEEKS DISTANCE | |
| TOTAL YEARLY DISTANCE | |

Monday **6** June		DISTANCE	
		TIME	
		PACE	
		HEART RATE	
		CALORIES	
Tuesday **7** June		DISTANCE	
		TIME	
		PACE	
		HEART RATE	
		CALORIES	
Wednesday **8** June		DISTANCE	
		TIME	
		PACE	
		HEART RATE	
		CALORIES	
Thursday **9** June		DISTANCE	
		TIME	
		PACE	
		HEART RATE	
		CALORIES	
Friday **10** June		DISTANCE	
		TIME	
		PACE	
		HEART RATE	
		CALORIES	
Saturday **11** June		DISTANCE	
		TIME	
		PACE	
		HEART RATE	
		CALORIES	
Sunday **12** June		DISTANCE	
		TIME	
		PACE	
		HEART RATE	
		CALORIES	

NOTES, ACHIEVEMENTS, EXTRA TRAINING

THIS WEEKS DISTANCE	
TOTAL YEARLY DISTANCE	

Monday **13** June		DISTANCE	
		TIME	
		PACE	
		HEART RATE	
		CALORIES	
Tuesday **14** June		DISTANCE	
		TIME	
		PACE	
		HEART RATE	
		CALORIES	
Wednesday **15** June		DISTANCE	
		TIME	
		PACE	
		HEART RATE	
		CALORIES	
Thursday **16** June		DISTANCE	
		TIME	
		PACE	
		HEART RATE	
		CALORIES	
Friday **17** June		DISTANCE	
		TIME	
		PACE	
		HEART RATE	
		CALORIES	
Saturday **18** June		DISTANCE	
		TIME	
		PACE	
		HEART RATE	
		CALORIES	
Sunday **19** June		DISTANCE	
		TIME	
		PACE	
		HEART RATE	
		CALORIES	

NOTES, ACHIEVEMENTS, EXTRA TRAINING

THIS WEEKS DISTANCE	
TOTAL YEARLY DISTANCE	

Monday **20** June		DISTANCE	
		TIME	
		PACE	
		HEART RATE	
		CALORIES	
Tuesday **21** June		DISTANCE	
		TIME	
		PACE	
		HEART RATE	
		CALORIES	
Wednesday **22** June		DISTANCE	
		TIME	
		PACE	
		HEART RATE	
		CALORIES	
Thursday **23** June		DISTANCE	
		TIME	
		PACE	
		HEART RATE	
		CALORIES	
Friday **24** June		DISTANCE	
		TIME	
		PACE	
		HEART RATE	
		CALORIES	
Saturday **25** June		DISTANCE	
		TIME	
		PACE	
		HEART RATE	
		CALORIES	
Sunday **26** June		DISTANCE	
		TIME	
		PACE	
		HEART RATE	
		CALORIES	

NOTES, ACHIEVEMENTS, EXTRA TRAINING

| THIS WEEKS DISTANCE | |
| TOTAL YEARLY DISTANCE | |

Monday **27** June		DISTANCE	
		TIME	
		PACE	
		HEART RATE	
		CALORIES	

Tuesday **28** June		DISTANCE	
		TIME	
		PACE	
		HEART RATE	
		CALORIES	

Wednesday **29** June		DISTANCE	
		TIME	
		PACE	
		HEART RATE	
		CALORIES	

Thursday **30** June		DISTANCE	
		TIME	
		PACE	
		HEART RATE	
		CALORIES	

Friday **1** July		DISTANCE	
		TIME	
		PACE	
		HEART RATE	
		CALORIES	

Saturday **2** July		DISTANCE	
		TIME	
		PACE	
		HEART RATE	
		CALORIES	

Sunday **3** July		DISTANCE	
		TIME	
		PACE	
		HEART RATE	
		CALORIES	

NOTES, ACHIEVEMENTS, EXTRA TRAINING

THIS WEEKS DISTANCE	
TOTAL YEARLY DISTANCE	

Monday 4 July		DISTANCE	
		TIME	
		PACE	
		HEART RATE	
		CALORIES	
Tuesday 5 July		DISTANCE	
		TIME	
		PACE	
		HEART RATE	
		CALORIES	
Wednesday 6 July		DISTANCE	
		TIME	
		PACE	
		HEART RATE	
		CALORIES	
Thursday 7 July		DISTANCE	
		TIME	
		PACE	
		HEART RATE	
		CALORIES	
Friday 8 July		DISTANCE	
		TIME	
		PACE	
		HEART RATE	
		CALORIES	
Saturday 9 July		DISTANCE	
		TIME	
		PACE	
		HEART RATE	
		CALORIES	
Sunday 10 July		DISTANCE	
		TIME	
		PACE	
		HEART RATE	
		CALORIES	

NOTES, ACHIEVEMENTS, EXTRA TRAINING

THIS WEEKS DISTANCE	
TOTAL YEARLY DISTANCE	

Monday **11** July		DISTANCE	
		TIME	
		PACE	
		HEART RATE	
		CALORIES	
Tuesday **12** July		DISTANCE	
		TIME	
		PACE	
		HEART RATE	
		CALORIES	
Wednesday **13** July		DISTANCE	
		TIME	
		PACE	
		HEART RATE	
		CALORIES	
Thursday **14** July		DISTANCE	
		TIME	
		PACE	
		HEART RATE	
		CALORIES	
Friday **15** July		DISTANCE	
		TIME	
		PACE	
		HEART RATE	
		CALORIES	
Saturday **16** July		DISTANCE	
		TIME	
		PACE	
		HEART RATE	
		CALORIES	
Sunday **17** July		DISTANCE	
		TIME	
		PACE	
		HEART RATE	
		CALORIES	

NOTES, ACHIEVEMENTS, EXTRA TRAINING

| THIS WEEKS DISTANCE | |
| TOTAL YEARLY DISTANCE | |

Monday **18** July		DISTANCE	
		TIME	
		PACE	
		HEART RATE	
		CALORIES	
Tuesday **19** July		DISTANCE	
		TIME	
		PACE	
		HEART RATE	
		CALORIES	
Wednesday **20** July		DISTANCE	
		TIME	
		PACE	
		HEART RATE	
		CALORIES	
Thursday **21** July		DISTANCE	
		TIME	
		PACE	
		HEART RATE	
		CALORIES	
Friday **22** July		DISTANCE	
		TIME	
		PACE	
		HEART RATE	
		CALORIES	
Saturday **23** July		DISTANCE	
		TIME	
		PACE	
		HEART RATE	
		CALORIES	
Sunday **24** July		DISTANCE	
		TIME	
		PACE	
		HEART RATE	
		CALORIES	

NOTES, ACHIEVEMENTS, EXTRA TRAINING

| THIS WEEKS DISTANCE | |
| TOTAL YEARLY DISTANCE | |

Monday **25** July		DISTANCE	
		TIME	
		PACE	
		HEART RATE	
		CALORIES	
Tuesday **26** July		DISTANCE	
		TIME	
		PACE	
		HEART RATE	
		CALORIES	
Wednesday **27** July		DISTANCE	
		TIME	
		PACE	
		HEART RATE	
		CALORIES	
Thursday **28** July		DISTANCE	
		TIME	
		PACE	
		HEART RATE	
		CALORIES	
Friday **29** July		DISTANCE	
		TIME	
		PACE	
		HEART RATE	
		CALORIES	
Saturday **30** July		DISTANCE	
		TIME	
		PACE	
		HEART RATE	
		CALORIES	
Sunday **31** July		DISTANCE	
		TIME	
		PACE	
		HEART RATE	
		CALORIES	

NOTES, ACHIEVEMENTS, EXTRA TRAINING

| THIS WEEKS DISTANCE | |
| TOTAL YEARLY DISTANCE | |

Monday 1 August		DISTANCE	
		TIME	
		PACE	
		HEART RATE	
		CALORIES	

Tuesday 2 August		DISTANCE	
		TIME	
		PACE	
		HEART RATE	
		CALORIES	

Wednesday 3 August		DISTANCE	
		TIME	
		PACE	
		HEART RATE	
		CALORIES	

Thursday 4 August		DISTANCE	
		TIME	
		PACE	
		HEART RATE	
		CALORIES	

Friday 5 August		DISTANCE	
		TIME	
		PACE	
		HEART RATE	
		CALORIES	

Saturday 6 August		DISTANCE	
		TIME	
		PACE	
		HEART RATE	
		CALORIES	

Sunday 7 August		DISTANCE	
		TIME	
		PACE	
		HEART RATE	
		CALORIES	

NOTES, ACHIEVEMENTS, EXTRA TRAINING

THIS WEEKS DISTANCE	
TOTAL YEARLY DISTANCE	

Monday **8** August		DISTANCE	
		TIME	
		PACE	
		HEART RATE	
		CALORIES	
Tuesday **9** August		DISTANCE	
		TIME	
		PACE	
		HEART RATE	
		CALORIES	
Wednesday **10** August		DISTANCE	
		TIME	
		PACE	
		HEART RATE	
		CALORIES	
Thursday **11** August		DISTANCE	
		TIME	
		PACE	
		HEART RATE	
		CALORIES	
Friday **12** August		DISTANCE	
		TIME	
		PACE	
		HEART RATE	
		CALORIES	
Saturday **13** August		DISTANCE	
		TIME	
		PACE	
		HEART RATE	
		CALORIES	
Sunday **14** August		DISTANCE	
		TIME	
		PACE	
		HEART RATE	
		CALORIES	

NOTES, ACHIEVEMENTS, EXTRA TRAINING

| THIS WEEKS DISTANCE | |
| TOTAL YEARLY DISTANCE | |

Monday **15** August		DISTANCE	
		TIME	
		PACE	
		HEART RATE	
		CALORIES	
Tuesday **16** August		DISTANCE	
		TIME	
		PACE	
		HEART RATE	
		CALORIES	
Wednesday **17** August		DISTANCE	
		TIME	
		PACE	
		HEART RATE	
		CALORIES	
Thursday **18** August		DISTANCE	
		TIME	
		PACE	
		HEART RATE	
		CALORIES	
Friday **19** August		DISTANCE	
		TIME	
		PACE	
		HEART RATE	
		CALORIES	
Saturday **20** August		DISTANCE	
		TIME	
		PACE	
		HEART RATE	
		CALORIES	
Sunday **21** August		DISTANCE	
		TIME	
		PACE	
		HEART RATE	
		CALORIES	

NOTES, ACHIEVEMENTS, EXTRA TRAINING

THIS WEEKS DISTANCE	
TOTAL YEARLY DISTANCE	

Monday **22** August		DISTANCE	
		TIME	
		PACE	
		HEART RATE	
		CALORIES	
Tuesday **23** August		DISTANCE	
		TIME	
		PACE	
		HEART RATE	
		CALORIES	
Wednesday **24** August		DISTANCE	
		TIME	
		PACE	
		HEART RATE	
		CALORIES	
Thursday **25** August		DISTANCE	
		TIME	
		PACE	
		HEART RATE	
		CALORIES	
Friday **26** August		DISTANCE	
		TIME	
		PACE	
		HEART RATE	
		CALORIES	
Saturday **27** August		DISTANCE	
		TIME	
		PACE	
		HEART RATE	
		CALORIES	
Sunday **28** August		DISTANCE	
		TIME	
		PACE	
		HEART RATE	
		CALORIES	

NOTES, ACHIEVEMENTS, EXTRA TRAINING

| THIS WEEKS DISTANCE | |
| TOTAL YEARLY DISTANCE | |

Monday 29 August		DISTANCE	
		TIME	
		PACE	
		HEART RATE	
		CALORIES	
Tuesday 30 August		DISTANCE	
		TIME	
		PACE	
		HEART RATE	
		CALORIES	
Wednesday 31 August		DISTANCE	
		TIME	
		PACE	
		HEART RATE	
		CALORIES	
Thursday 1 September		DISTANCE	
		TIME	
		PACE	
		HEART RATE	
		CALORIES	
Friday 2 September		DISTANCE	
		TIME	
		PACE	
		HEART RATE	
		CALORIES	
Saturday 3 September		DISTANCE	
		TIME	
		PACE	
		HEART RATE	
		CALORIES	
Sunday 4 September		DISTANCE	
		TIME	
		PACE	
		HEART RATE	
		CALORIES	

NOTES, ACHIEVEMENTS, EXTRA TRAINING

| THIS WEEKS DISTANCE | |
| TOTAL YEARLY DISTANCE | |

Monday 5 September		DISTANCE	
		TIME	
		PACE	
		HEART RATE	
		CALORIES	
Tuesday 6 September		DISTANCE	
		TIME	
		PACE	
		HEART RATE	
		CALORIES	
Wednesday 7 September		DISTANCE	
		TIME	
		PACE	
		HEART RATE	
		CALORIES	
Thursday 8 September		DISTANCE	
		TIME	
		PACE	
		HEART RATE	
		CALORIES	
Friday 9 September		DISTANCE	
		TIME	
		PACE	
		HEART RATE	
		CALORIES	
Saturday 10 September		DISTANCE	
		TIME	
		PACE	
		HEART RATE	
		CALORIES	
Sunday 11 September		DISTANCE	
		TIME	
		PACE	
		HEART RATE	
		CALORIES	

NOTES, ACHIEVEMENTS, EXTRA TRAINING

| THIS WEEKS DISTANCE | |
| TOTAL YEARLY DISTANCE | |

Monday **12** September		DISTANCE	
		TIME	
		PACE	
		HEART RATE	
		CALORIES	
Tuesday **13** September		DISTANCE	
		TIME	
		PACE	
		HEART RATE	
		CALORIES	
Wednesday **14** September		DISTANCE	
		TIME	
		PACE	
		HEART RATE	
		CALORIES	
Thursday **15** September		DISTANCE	
		TIME	
		PACE	
		HEART RATE	
		CALORIES	
Friday **16** September		DISTANCE	
		TIME	
		PACE	
		HEART RATE	
		CALORIES	
Saturday **17** September		DISTANCE	
		TIME	
		PACE	
		HEART RATE	
		CALORIES	
Sunday **18** September		DISTANCE	
		TIME	
		PACE	
		HEART RATE	
		CALORIES	

NOTES, ACHIEVEMENTS, EXTRA TRAINING

| THIS WEEKS DISTANCE | |
| TOTAL YEARLY DISTANCE | |

Monday **19** September		DISTANCE	
		TIME	
		PACE	
		HEART RATE	
		CALORIES	

Tuesday **20** September		DISTANCE	
		TIME	
		PACE	
		HEART RATE	
		CALORIES	

Wednesday **21** September		DISTANCE	
		TIME	
		PACE	
		HEART RATE	
		CALORIES	

Thursday **22** September		DISTANCE	
		TIME	
		PACE	
		HEART RATE	
		CALORIES	

Friday **23** September		DISTANCE	
		TIME	
		PACE	
		HEART RATE	
		CALORIES	

Saturday **24** September		DISTANCE	
		TIME	
		PACE	
		HEART RATE	
		CALORIES	

Sunday **25** September		DISTANCE	
		TIME	
		PACE	
		HEART RATE	
		CALORIES	

NOTES, ACHIEVEMENTS, EXTRA TRAINING

| THIS WEEKS DISTANCE | |
| TOTAL YEARLY DISTANCE | |

Monday **26** September		DISTANCE	
		TIME	
		PACE	
		HEART RATE	
		CALORIES	
Tuesday **27** September		DISTANCE	
		TIME	
		PACE	
		HEART RATE	
		CALORIES	
Wednesday **28** September		DISTANCE	
		TIME	
		PACE	
		HEART RATE	
		CALORIES	
Thursday **29** September		DISTANCE	
		TIME	
		PACE	
		HEART RATE	
		CALORIES	
Friday **30** September		DISTANCE	
		TIME	
		PACE	
		HEART RATE	
		CALORIES	
Saturday **1** October		DISTANCE	
		TIME	
		PACE	
		HEART RATE	
		CALORIES	
Sunday **2** October		DISTANCE	
		TIME	
		PACE	
		HEART RATE	
		CALORIES	

NOTES, ACHIEVEMENTS, EXTRA TRAINING

| THIS WEEKS DISTANCE | |
| TOTAL YEARLY DISTANCE | |

Monday **3** October		DISTANCE	
		TIME	
		PACE	
		HEART RATE	
		CALORIES	

Tuesday **4** October		DISTANCE	
		TIME	
		PACE	
		HEART RATE	
		CALORIES	

Wednesday **5** October		DISTANCE	
		TIME	
		PACE	
		HEART RATE	
		CALORIES	

Thursday **6** October		DISTANCE	
		TIME	
		PACE	
		HEART RATE	
		CALORIES	

Friday **7** October		DISTANCE	
		TIME	
		PACE	
		HEART RATE	
		CALORIES	

Saturday **8** October		DISTANCE	
		TIME	
		PACE	
		HEART RATE	
		CALORIES	

Sunday **9** October		DISTANCE	
		TIME	
		PACE	
		HEART RATE	
		CALORIES	

NOTES, ACHIEVEMENTS, EXTRA TRAINING

| THIS WEEKS DISTANCE | |
| TOTAL YEARLY DISTANCE | |

Monday **10** October		DISTANCE	
		TIME	
		PACE	
		HEART RATE	
		CALORIES	
Tuesday **11** October		DISTANCE	
		TIME	
		PACE	
		HEART RATE	
		CALORIES	
Wednesday **12** October		DISTANCE	
		TIME	
		PACE	
		HEART RATE	
		CALORIES	
Thursday **13** October		DISTANCE	
		TIME	
		PACE	
		HEART RATE	
		CALORIES	
Friday **14** October		DISTANCE	
		TIME	
		PACE	
		HEART RATE	
		CALORIES	
Saturday **15** October		DISTANCE	
		TIME	
		PACE	
		HEART RATE	
		CALORIES	
Sunday **16** October		DISTANCE	
		TIME	
		PACE	
		HEART RATE	
		CALORIES	

NOTES, ACHIEVEMENTS, EXTRA TRAINING

THIS WEEKS DISTANCE	
TOTAL YEARLY DISTANCE	

Monday **17** October		DISTANCE	
		TIME	
		PACE	
		HEART RATE	
		CALORIES	

Tuesday **18** October		DISTANCE	
		TIME	
		PACE	
		HEART RATE	
		CALORIES	

Wednesday **19** October		DISTANCE	
		TIME	
		PACE	
		HEART RATE	
		CALORIES	

Thursday **20** October		DISTANCE	
		TIME	
		PACE	
		HEART RATE	
		CALORIES	

Friday **21** October		DISTANCE	
		TIME	
		PACE	
		HEART RATE	
		CALORIES	

Saturday **22** October		DISTANCE	
		TIME	
		PACE	
		HEART RATE	
		CALORIES	

Sunday **23** October		DISTANCE	
		TIME	
		PACE	
		HEART RATE	
		CALORIES	

NOTES, ACHIEVEMENTS, EXTRA TRAINING

THIS WEEKS DISTANCE	
TOTAL YEARLY DISTANCE	

Monday **24** October		DISTANCE	
		TIME	
		PACE	
		HEART RATE	
		CALORIES	
Tuesday **25** October		DISTANCE	
		TIME	
		PACE	
		HEART RATE	
		CALORIES	
Wednesday **26** October		DISTANCE	
		TIME	
		PACE	
		HEART RATE	
		CALORIES	
Thursday **27** October		DISTANCE	
		TIME	
		PACE	
		HEART RATE	
		CALORIES	
Friday **28** October		DISTANCE	
		TIME	
		PACE	
		HEART RATE	
		CALORIES	
Saturday **29** October		DISTANCE	
		TIME	
		PACE	
		HEART RATE	
		CALORIES	
Sunday **30** October		DISTANCE	
		TIME	
		PACE	
		HEART RATE	
		CALORIES	

NOTES, ACHIEVEMENTS, EXTRA TRAINING

| THIS WEEKS DISTANCE | |
| TOTAL YEARLY DISTANCE | |

Monday **31** October		DISTANCE	
		TIME	
		PACE	
		HEART RATE	
		CALORIES	
Tuesday **1** November		DISTANCE	
		TIME	
		PACE	
		HEART RATE	
		CALORIES	
Wednesday **2** November		DISTANCE	
		TIME	
		PACE	
		HEART RATE	
		CALORIES	
Thursday **3** November		DISTANCE	
		TIME	
		PACE	
		HEART RATE	
		CALORIES	
Friday **4** November		DISTANCE	
		TIME	
		PACE	
		HEART RATE	
		CALORIES	
Saturday **5** November		DISTANCE	
		TIME	
		PACE	
		HEART RATE	
		CALORIES	
Sunday **6** November		DISTANCE	
		TIME	
		PACE	
		HEART RATE	
		CALORIES	

NOTES, ACHIEVEMENTS, EXTRA TRAINING

| THIS WEEKS DISTANCE | |
| TOTAL YEARLY DISTANCE | |

Monday **7** November		DISTANCE	
		TIME	
		PACE	
		HEART RATE	
		CALORIES	
Tuesday **8** November		DISTANCE	
		TIME	
		PACE	
		HEART RATE	
		CALORIES	
Wednesday **9** November		DISTANCE	
		TIME	
		PACE	
		HEART RATE	
		CALORIES	
Thursday **10** November		DISTANCE	
		TIME	
		PACE	
		HEART RATE	
		CALORIES	
Friday **11** November		DISTANCE	
		TIME	
		PACE	
		HEART RATE	
		CALORIES	
Saturday **12** November		DISTANCE	
		TIME	
		PACE	
		HEART RATE	
		CALORIES	
Sunday **13** November		DISTANCE	
		TIME	
		PACE	
		HEART RATE	
		CALORIES	

NOTES, ACHIEVEMENTS, EXTRA TRAINING

| THIS WEEKS DISTANCE | |
| TOTAL YEARLY DISTANCE | |

Monday **14** November		DISTANCE	
		TIME	
		PACE	
		HEART RATE	
		CALORIES	
Tuesday **15** November		DISTANCE	
		TIME	
		PACE	
		HEART RATE	
		CALORIES	
Wednesday **16** November		DISTANCE	
		TIME	
		PACE	
		HEART RATE	
		CALORIES	
Thursday **17** November		DISTANCE	
		TIME	
		PACE	
		HEART RATE	
		CALORIES	
Friday **18** November		DISTANCE	
		TIME	
		PACE	
		HEART RATE	
		CALORIES	
Saturday **19** November		DISTANCE	
		TIME	
		PACE	
		HEART RATE	
		CALORIES	
Sunday **20** November		DISTANCE	
		TIME	
		PACE	
		HEART RATE	
		CALORIES	

NOTES, ACHIEVEMENTS, EXTRA TRAINING

THIS WEEKS DISTANCE	
TOTAL YEARLY DISTANCE	

Monday **21** November		DISTANCE	
		TIME	
		PACE	
		HEART RATE	
		CALORIES	
Tuesday **22** November		DISTANCE	
		TIME	
		PACE	
		HEART RATE	
		CALORIES	
Wednesday **23** November		DISTANCE	
		TIME	
		PACE	
		HEART RATE	
		CALORIES	
Thursday **24** November		DISTANCE	
		TIME	
		PACE	
		HEART RATE	
		CALORIES	
Friday **25** November		DISTANCE	
		TIME	
		PACE	
		HEART RATE	
		CALORIES	
Saturday **26** November		DISTANCE	
		TIME	
		PACE	
		HEART RATE	
		CALORIES	
Sunday **27** November		DISTANCE	
		TIME	
		PACE	
		HEART RATE	
		CALORIES	

NOTES, ACHIEVEMENTS, EXTRA TRAINING

THIS WEEKS DISTANCE	
TOTAL YEARLY DISTANCE	

Monday **28** November		DISTANCE	
		TIME	
		PACE	
		HEART RATE	
		CALORIES	

Tuesday **29** November		DISTANCE	
		TIME	
		PACE	
		HEART RATE	
		CALORIES	

Wednesday **30** November		DISTANCE	
		TIME	
		PACE	
		HEART RATE	
		CALORIES	

Thursday **1** December		DISTANCE	
		TIME	
		PACE	
		HEART RATE	
		CALORIES	

Friday **2** December		DISTANCE	
		TIME	
		PACE	
		HEART RATE	
		CALORIES	

Saturday **3** December		DISTANCE	
		TIME	
		PACE	
		HEART RATE	
		CALORIES	

Sunday **4** December		DISTANCE	
		TIME	
		PACE	
		HEART RATE	
		CALORIES	

NOTES, ACHIEVEMENTS, EXTRA TRAINING

| THIS WEEKS DISTANCE | |
| TOTAL YEARLY DISTANCE | |

Monday **5** December		DISTANCE	
		TIME	
		PACE	
		HEART RATE	
		CALORIES	
Tuesday **6** December		DISTANCE	
		TIME	
		PACE	
		HEART RATE	
		CALORIES	
Wednesday **7** December		DISTANCE	
		TIME	
		PACE	
		HEART RATE	
		CALORIES	
Thursday **8** December		DISTANCE	
		TIME	
		PACE	
		HEART RATE	
		CALORIES	
Friday **9** December		DISTANCE	
		TIME	
		PACE	
		HEART RATE	
		CALORIES	
Saturday **10** December		DISTANCE	
		TIME	
		PACE	
		HEART RATE	
		CALORIES	
Sunday **11** December		DISTANCE	
		TIME	
		PACE	
		HEART RATE	
		CALORIES	

NOTES, ACHIEVEMENTS, EXTRA TRAINING

THIS WEEKS DISTANCE	
TOTAL YEARLY DISTANCE	

Monday **12** December		DISTANCE	
		TIME	
		PACE	
		HEART RATE	
		CALORIES	
Tuesday **13** December		DISTANCE	
		TIME	
		PACE	
		HEART RATE	
		CALORIES	
Wednesday **14** December		DISTANCE	
		TIME	
		PACE	
		HEART RATE	
		CALORIES	
Thursday **15** December		DISTANCE	
		TIME	
		PACE	
		HEART RATE	
		CALORIES	
Friday **16** December		DISTANCE	
		TIME	
		PACE	
		HEART RATE	
		CALORIES	
Saturday **17** December		DISTANCE	
		TIME	
		PACE	
		HEART RATE	
		CALORIES	
Sunday **18** December		DISTANCE	
		TIME	
		PACE	
		HEART RATE	
		CALORIES	

NOTES, ACHIEVEMENTS, EXTRA TRAINING

THIS WEEKS DISTANCE	
TOTAL YEARLY DISTANCE	

Monday **19** December		DISTANCE	
		TIME	
		PACE	
		HEART RATE	
		CALORIES	
Tuesday **20** December		DISTANCE	
		TIME	
		PACE	
		HEART RATE	
		CALORIES	
Wednesday **21** December		DISTANCE	
		TIME	
		PACE	
		HEART RATE	
		CALORIES	
Thursday **22** December		DISTANCE	
		TIME	
		PACE	
		HEART RATE	
		CALORIES	
Friday **23** December		DISTANCE	
		TIME	
		PACE	
		HEART RATE	
		CALORIES	
Saturday **24** December		DISTANCE	
		TIME	
		PACE	
		HEART RATE	
		CALORIES	
Sunday **25** December		DISTANCE	
		TIME	
		PACE	
		HEART RATE	
		CALORIES	

NOTES, ACHIEVEMENTS, EXTRA TRAINING

THIS WEEKS DISTANCE	
TOTAL YEARLY DISTANCE	

Monday **26** December		DISTANCE	
		TIME	
		PACE	
		HEART RATE	
		CALORIES	
Tuesday **27** December		DISTANCE	
		TIME	
		PACE	
		HEART RATE	
		CALORIES	
Wednesday **28** December		DISTANCE	
		TIME	
		PACE	
		HEART RATE	
		CALORIES	
Thursday **29** December		DISTANCE	
		TIME	
		PACE	
		HEART RATE	
		CALORIES	
Friday **30** December		DISTANCE	
		TIME	
		PACE	
		HEART RATE	
		CALORIES	
Saturday **31** December		DISTANCE	
		TIME	
		PACE	
		HEART RATE	
		CALORIES	
Sunday **1** January		DISTANCE	
		TIME	
		PACE	
		HEART RATE	
		CALORIES	

NOTES, ACHIEVEMENTS, EXTRA TRAINING

| THIS WEEKS DISTANCE | |
| TOTAL YEARLY DISTANCE | |

Total Distance Run	
Longest Run	
Number of Runs	
Number of Races Run	
Total Distance (Race)	
Quickest Pace (Race)	
Best Placement in a Race	
Average Race Placement	
Longest Weekly Distance	
Longest Monthly Distance	

YEARLY REFLECTION

Use this space to reflect on your year! You decide what you would like to reflect on. Some suggestion topics include:

- Proudest Moments
- Areas in which you saw improvement
- Areas to focus on for next year
- Favourite runs
- Tips for yourself
- Favourite Races
- Everything and anything else to do with running

NOTES

DATE	NOTE

DATE	NOTE

NOTES

DATE	NOTE

DATE	NOTE

NOTES

DATE	NOTE

DATE	NOTE

NOTES

DATE	NOTE

DATE	NOTE

NOTES

DATE	NOTE

DATE	NOTE

NOTES

DATE	NOTE

DATE	NOTE

NOTES

DATE	NOTE

DATE	NOTE

NOTES

DATE	NOTE

DATE	NOTE

NOTES

DATE	NOTE

DATE	NOTE

NOTES

DATE	NOTE

DATE	NOTE

NOTES

DATE	NOTE

DATE	NOTE

Thankyou for your purchase!

If you get the chance, we would love an honest review on the location in which you purchased this book. We are a small business that appreciates every review!

Made in United States
North Haven, CT
14 January 2022

14766195R00067